The Gift of Less

9/18

To Kate
Blessing always
marie

By Maria Aponte

Author of "Transitions of a Nuyorican Cinderella"

The Gift of Loss

Copyright © 2016 by Maria Aponte

Cover art and design by Mia Roman Hernandez
Author photo by George Malave
Published by Aponte-Gonzalez Productions

Printed in USA

Categories
Nuyorican Experience
Puerto Rican Women Studies
Women Studies
Memoir

Dedication

For Rosie & Victor

From Your Daughter

Maria

To my Bobby you are my heart.

Table of Contents

Part One:

My Heart Beats With My Father's Clave Beat...

Part Two:

The day I forgave my parents...

Part Three:

There are too many people...

Part Four

My Nuyorican Puerta & Open Mics

Part Five

In the end no matter what, you have...

Thank you

About the Artist

About the Author

Author's Notes

Part One

My heart beats with my father's clave beat.

Rhythmic movements of bloodlines

that cannot be erased.

In Rhythm

My father was a man of medium height, brown complexion. Eyes the size of saucers, sparkling with energy, pupils constantly moving, observant, trying to swallow the world in an instant, an arched eyebrow frown curled into an arrow pointing nowhere

Wiggly lines forming across clear skin smelling like English Leather cologne, polished fingernails, dark chocolate suit, small gold pinkie ring like a flashlight, he would twirl my mother, her small waist, taffeta dress, and they would dance. Swinging, chasing silhouettes in the mirrors of blue-red faded dance halls. He looked to be taking her in, swallowing her whole.

I was a little girl and wanted these moments to last forever.

They would not.

Instructions

1. When your Father picks you up, pay attention to where you're going.
2. Don't tell him anything about home; its none of his business.
3. Don't take anything from him. I don't trust him.
4. Remember everything you see. When you come home I want to know everything.

Pause.

Look.

"Maria, did you hear me? "

"Yes Mami."

"Good, now what did I just say?"

Pause.

Look.

Respond.

Tattoo

Whenever I saw my dad, he always cried with a shaky voice that would rattle like rain hitting a windowpane. I would stand apart from him as if he were contagious, remembering my instructions. So when he cried, I didn't. He knew he couldn't give me anything.

Whenever I saw my dad, he would shout out to anyone that would listen, *"¡Esta es mi hija!"* This is my daughter!" Sometimes he would point to the sky and shout as if the gods could hear him. One day, he showed me the tattoo on his left arm, rolling up his sleeve and proudly pointing at the blue-ink letters that said, *"Mi Hija."* The tattoo had my birth date.

"I had it done the day you were born," he told me. I looked and, as instructed, didn't say anything. All I could think was: *Why didn't he put my name?*

Magical Secrets

Saturday visits by my father were well organized and orchestrated. After my parents separated, Mami and I lived in El Barrio, Dad in the Bronx.

My father was not allowed to take me out of the neighborhood. So his Saturday visits consisted of taking me to nearby Jefferson Park on 115th street and 1st avenue. My mother would give my father very specific directions on how to take me to the park, her most important being: "Vic, don't buy her too much candy, then she won't eat dinner!"

My father would nod his head several times and mutter, "Yes, Rosie," and off we'd go to Jefferson Park. First we just walked around, then he would put me on the swings for a while and later buy me too little candy. Then it was back upstairs to my house—all in a total of two to three hours.

As I said, the visits were well organized and orchestrated.

But on one particular Saturday in the summer, when I was seven-years old, my paternal grandmother phones Mami and asks if she could see, me instead of my father just taking me to the local park. Mami isn't too crazy about the itinerary change, but gives her approval. She turns to my father and barks a new instruction.

"Okay Vic, you can take her to see your Mother but have her back here before dinner!"

My father readily agrees, grabs my hand and we head out the door. As we're walking down the stairs he starts whistling. I look up at him and he smiles.

On our way to the 116th subway station on Lexington Avenue, my father stops and tells me, "Maria I want to show you something before I take you to my Mami's home today okay?"

I look at him. He smiles. I smile back. "Okay," I say.

"Great, let's catch the train!"

We board the No. 6 train going downtown. My father is whistling again and I start wondering where we're going. I ask him a bunch of questions but he gives me the same answer all the time.

"It's a surprise."

"What kind?"

"It's a surprise."

My father is a musician, a drummer, a *timbalero*. As the train chugs along, he plays an imaginary beat on his thighs, a Bap, Bap matching the clangs of the train. I close my eyes and play along with him. When I got older, I would realize that his music was his like his own private language, his way of talking to the dancers. Lost between his timbales he ruled. Until the lights came up and the soft red/blue lights shifted to harsh reminders that his life was not a happy musical.

***

By the time we reach downtown Manhattan and hop on the F train heading to Brooklyn, I'm feeling excited. Back then, in 1964, all the trains were painted gunmetal green with straw seats that were often broken, and when I sat on them I got straw stuck in my butt. The ceiling fans turned slowly and blew out more dirt than air. But today I'm just taking it all in, my first time doing something different with my father except what Mami ordered. Going to a "mystery place!"

The minutes zoom by and I notice that my father keeps looking out the window, as if waiting for something. Suddenly, he grabs my hand and starts running, and I'm running right with him. We race up the aisle and through the door to the space in between the subway cars, held together by linked chains, with just enough space to carefully step from one car to the next. My father holds my hand tightly as the hot wind hits my face.

We make it to the next car, and I continue to follow my father, who's still looking for something. He finds an unlocked door to one of the rooms where the train conductor works, using a long metal on a control board to open and close the train doors. The room is empty and the size of a small closet. Another mystery place! Dad picks me up and opens the window.

"Close your eyes," he instructs. I do.

"Keep them closed and wait."

I nod, having no idea what we're doing. All I know is that my Dad and I are like two kids on an adventure. As the train makes a sharp turn, I feel the sun hit my face, the light visible behind my eyelids.

"Maria, look!" he says.

I open my eyes and see the Cyclone roller coaster for the first time in my life.

"It's Coney Island!"

Dad smiles. "That's right, *mi hija.*"

I stare in amazement at other rides like the Wonder Wheel as the train draws nearer to its destination. I had never been to Coney Island. And now here it was, looming like a land out of a fairy-tale.

I wrinkle my nose. "What is that smell?"

My father starts laughing. "It's the ocean!"

The ocean!

Up until then, I had never been to the ocean, and I had yet to visit Puerto Rico, where my parents were born.

When the F train pulls into the Stillwell Avenue station, the smell of hotdogs and popcorn hit my senses. All around me people are laughing. I'm so excited I could burst.

My father looks at his watch. "Okay nena, we have to get back on the train and go back to the Bronx so you can see your Grandmother!"

I point to the noise and laughter. "But we're not going there?"

"No. Remember, I have to get you home for before dinner?"

"But—"

"One day."

I sigh and decide not to make a scene. That would go against every instruction Mami gave me.

The train pulls away and the noises fade. I sigh again at the end of my magical trip. My first time to Brooklyn. My first adventure with Dad.

***

An hour later, we're back in the Bronx and I'm smiling again. I'm going to see Abuela! I always felt that her apartment at 1163 Simpson Street was like a palace compared to where I lived in El Barrio. The building foyer had wider hallways and shiny black and white square tiles on the floor. Abuela lived on the second floor in what was then called a railroad apartment, which meant all the rooms were lined up in a row.

Abuela's apartment wasn't just any apartment. It was also the place where folks in the neighborhood came to see her with their personal problems, illnesses, broken marriages, and, the list went on and on. My grandmother was a *Curandera*, a spiritual healer who gave spiritual readings, and Saturdays were her busiest day. She had a special room where she met with people and to which I had never dared venture. The long hallway to the room scared me, as if it was occupied by ghosts, watching me, following me.

But this Saturday I'm full of energy! I had just experienced a glimpse of the dreamlike Coney Island, a place I swore I would revisit when "I grew up." So when I arrived at Abuela's, I decided I was now brave enough to finally venture enter her special room.

I open the door, which is slightly ajar. I peek in and see Abuela with a cigar in her mouth, holding seashells in her hands. Another woman is sitting in a chair directly across from her, crying. Grocery bags are on the floor, as if she had just came from shopping. The saints on

Abuela's altar have candles lit in front of them, casting shadows on the wall. The altar goes from floor to ceiling. I'm frozen, fascinated at my Abuela who at that moment doesn't look like my Abuela. She takes the seashells and throws them on the floor. They make the shape of a star. The woman with the grocery bags stares at them. Abuela puffs on her cigar.

That's quite enough, I tell myself, and begin backing away into the hallway, right into my grandfather.

"Muchacha ¿qué tú haces aquí?" he asks.

I'm tongue-tied and he takes me by the hand to the kitchen, where he gives my usual slice of pound cake with milk. As I'm finishing my milk in comes Abuela.

"*Mija!*" she says, hugging me. I take a deep breath. *She doesn't smell like cigars!*

Abuela has a twinkle in her eye and tells me that she saw me by the door. My face turns red as a beet and she hugs me again. She then bends down and whispers in my ear: "*Un día cuando tu seas grandecita vamos hablar de muchas cosas.*"

I stare at her. What does she want to talk about, and why does she want to wait until I'm bigger? What does she know?

My father, who is standing nearby, looks at his watch and yells that it's time to go. As I get up, my grandmother tells me to wait as she goes into her bedroom. When she returns, she hands me a bag.

"*Te hice un traje.* A pretty dress for you."
Her eyes are shiny with tears.

"Gracias, Abuela," I say and hug her back.

"Time to go," says Dad.

Back in East Harlem, a quiet has settled over my father and me. According to the newly orchestrated plan we are now two hours overdue. When we reach the top of the stairs to my apartment, Mami is already at the door waiting, most likely had been looking out the window all that time. Her hands are on her hips.

"Vic, aside from your Mother's, where else did you take Maria?"

"Rosie, I took her to see her Grandmother that's all," he says, sounding tired.

Mami stares at me. Should I say anything?

After a few long seconds, she turns to my father and says, "Well, next time call if you're bringing her back late. I was worried!"

"Okay, Rosie."

And with that, Dad kisses my cheek and ask, "You had a good time today?"

I smile and exclaim, "Yes!"

Mami frowns and rushes my father out the door. I start walking to my bedroom.

"Maria!"

I turn around. "Yes, Mami?"

"Where did your father take you today?"

"To Grandma's house, Mami."

She tries staring me down and realizes I'm not going to say anything more.

"Go to your room and change and get ready for dinner," she says.

In my bedroom, I take off my sneakers, and close my eyes. Inhaling deeply, I smell the Atlantic Ocean, and see star-shaped seashells on Abuela's floor.

The Big Deal

Graduation from the eighth grade was a big deal that June of 1971. Mami went into overdrive transforming our little two-bedroom, bathtub-in-the-kitchen apartment into a place befitting royalty. After all, her daughter was not only graduating from grade school, but would be going into high school in September. Such an occasion called for Mami to man the telephone as the "Lady in Charge." She invited all her friends to attend the festivities, all the way out from New Jersey, Long Island, and that grand, new complex in the Bronx, Co-op City!

The apartment was redone from top to bottom with splashes of pride. New wallpaper with a velvet pattern, purchased on sale at

Martin's Paint on Third Avenue and Eighty-fifth Street, hid the ugly water stains on the living room wall. New curtains adorned the windows, and new bedspreads covered the beds, all handcrafted by my mother. She was a great seamstress, and had put in some serious overtime on the Singer sewing machine, working her hands until late at night, the steady rhythm of the sewing machine like a lull-a-bye that put me to sleep.

The "Big Day" comes. Head high, Mami marches me down the street to St. Paul's Church on 117th street and Park Avenue, my white and gold cap and gown glowing in the morning sunshine. A small army of friends and family are there, dressed to the nines. The mass soars with passion and I receive awards for academic achievement, as well as my diploma.

Like I said, it was a big deal.

After the ceremony, we go back to the house for the "Big Party." The record player is on full blast as salsa music bounces off the new wallpaper. Mounds of food are passed around: *pernil, arroz con gandules, pollo frito, ensalada de aguacate.* I lose count of the hugs and congratulations I receive, gracias I say. I hear a knock on the door.

"Whoever is near the door open it!" my mother yells from the kitchen.

Suddenly, the laughter and talking becomes lower.

"Who is it?" Mami asks.

"Rosie, its Victor!" someone replies.

I'm not in the kitchen to see her face, but I know my mother and could feel her. Coiled. Ready to snap. "I'll be right there," she says.

Wiping her hands on her apron, she walks to the door. Before the graduation, my mother had insisted that my father wouldn't be allowed to come to the party. But her tone changed when she saw him.

"Victor, what are you doing here?"

Taking off his sunglasses he replies, "I came to give my daughter her graduation present."

Mami is taken aback, "Her graduation present?"

"Yes."

She pauses and looks him over. "Wait here."

I'm called over and told that my father has a present for me. I expect him to come inside, but the Lady in Charge resumes her command and tells him, "I don't want you in here. You can give her whatever you bought out in the hallway."

Barely a whisper could be heard as father and daughter go out the door. We stand by the hallway window, which offers a grand view of the garbage in the building's backyard. For a while neither of us speak; the sounds of silence, a language all its own. When he does finally talk, his voice is shaky. "I wasn't going to let today go by without giving you your graduation present."

My father reaches into the side pocket of his jacket, pulls out a gold box and hands it to me. It's the first time Papi has given me something besides candy. I open the box. Inside is a gold bracelet with little pearls. More silence. I can't think of what to say.

He takes the bracelet and tries to put it on my wrist, but his hands are shaking too much. I put my hand out to let him know it's okay. I place the bracelet back in the box, and thank him. He gazes at me with those big cow eyes of his and tells me how much he loves me and how he wishes he could give me more, and...

Suddenly my mother's voice rings out, looking for us. "We're right here, Rosie!" my father says.

He pecks me on the cheek and puts his sunglasses back on. I know better than to ask when I would see him again. I've learned. He takes his time going down the stairs.

I take my gold box and go back to the graduation party.

Bitter Sweet Sixteen

It's the morning of my Sweet Sixteen and Mami has graduated from Lady in Charge to General of "Operation Maria." Four years ago, Mami was diagnosed with Scleroderma, and doctors were not optimistic about a cure.

But despite being wheelchair bound, she is determined to have today's celebration run smoothly and efficiently. When the black wall phone rings, she gets up and walks painfully to pick it up. It's important that she answer. Only the General of Operation Maria knows who's been invited and who hasn't.

Out of breath she picks up the phone. "Hello, City Morgue!"

Her laughter quickly turns apologetic. *"Hola, Doña Carmen."* It's my grandmother, aka Chief Financial Officer of "Operation Maria." I smile to myself. It takes a lot to get Mami to change her usual way of communicating: which was straight forward and curt. Her body language shifts as she listens to Abuela.

"I'll be damned. Your father wants to come and perform at your Sweet Sixteen! Knowing him, he'll come drunk! I don't need this shit!"

My mother could curse like a sailor one minute and say a Hail Mary in the next. That was Mami, all 4 feet 11 inches of her; a battering ram ready to run you down. I should know. I'd been battered and rammed quite a few times already. I could see that her fuse was getting ready to blow, so I kept out of the way. Slowly pulling the nearest kitchen chair over, she picks up her address book, and thumbs through her alphabetized listing, ready to begin dialing the troops.

Pausing, she recovers her General's voice and hands me a list of "Things for Maria to Do," among them to pick up my own birthday cake from the Valencia Bakery on 116th Street and Lexington Avenue. I don't mind, though. After all, it is my cake. As I get ready to leave, I hear Mami's voice on the phone.

"Hello Paula? You are not going to believe this! I just got off the phone with Victor's mother and he told her to call me to let me know he wants to come and play at Maria's party! Can you believe this shit! The man, never did anything for her and no..."

I don't need to hear the rest; I already know the conversation by heart. I close the front door and leave.

Despite the drama, I'm thrilled about my Sweet Sixteen. My *capias*—the little party favors that get pinned on guests' dresses or lapels at weddings and parties—were handmade by Abuela. My best friend at the time, Rosemary, and I were going to be identically dressed in powered blue bell bottom pants with white platform heels.

And I was finally going to listen to my own music! I couldn't wait to hear "Gotta Get A Knutt," by New Birth. Mami hated the album cover. "Why did they have to take a picture of a dozen eggs painted black?" Our musical tastes had by now traveled in decidedly different directions. My mother grew up in the Palladium era, the age of the big bands like Tito Rodriguez and Machito playing mambos and cha-chas. But it was my birthday and she had said, "Whatever you want, Maria—for today."

Amidst the chaos of family and family friends calling to say they were on their way, asking for the millionth time where exactly the place was and can you give the address again? Mami and I got dressed. Helping to get her ready while she sat in a wheelchair was challenging, but after years of taking care of her we had established a routine.

Dressed, perfumed, red lipstick in place, she takes a final look in the compact mirror. "If I have to see your Father tonight, I may be in a wheelchair but I can still look good!" Satisfied, she snaps the compact case and returns it into her evening bag that hasn't seen the outside world in a while.

Next came the stairs. We live in a walk up tenement building and maneuvering the wheelchair has become yet another part of our routine. Thankfully, a few of my cousins had arrived early to help, and with explicit instructions from the General of "Operation Maria", they carefully carry my mother down the stairs.

In good fashion, our entourage walks to the social club. Then came the *real* stairs. Like most social clubs of the period, they had a very long flight of stairs to climb. My cousins stare at the looming steps and have a quick discussion as to who will take the front of the wheel chair and who will take the back. Inhaling deeply, they begin the ascent. I follow carrying all sorts of different bags and avoid looking at my mother. I knew she hated to be dependent on others, but what can you do?

After a half-hour or so, the party's in full swing. We only have one record player and I have my cousin play "Gotta Get a Knutt" by New Birth over and over again. Mami is totally embarrassed by the lyrics "Charlie says he loves my Good N' Plenty..." and I pretend I don't see her. After all, it's my party and I'll do what I want to, right?

The adults are just sitting around and glancing at their watches, whispering what I suspect is a string of *bochinches* about whether my father would show up. Abuela is at the party, with my Father's sister.

After wearing out the New Birth album, I get ready to cut the cake, filled with pineapple chunks and enough sugar to keep every dentist in New York happily busy. All of a sudden, there's a commotion at the entrance. Everyone turns to look and in strolls my father carrying his timbales and accompanied by a guy with a trumpet and a woman lugging a conga drum. His band. I stand there, mouth open. I had never seen my father perform, although rumor had it that my parents first met each other at a dance at the Palladium. Now here he was, cuddling his timbales like an infant. The adults are shocked, having taken bets that he wouldn't show up.

Papi beams, his brown eyes as big as an ocean. "Maria! *Mi hija!* My daughter! I came to play for your birthday!"

The room is quiet. Abuela has a small smile on her face. Mami looks like she could shoot daggers out of her eyes. Papi looks at Mami and gasps. It's the first time he's seen her in a wheelchair. Mami didn't want him to know that she was sick.

He goes to her. "Rosie, are you okay?"

"I'm fine Victor!" Seeing that she's getting defensive, he changes the subject and asks where he could set up. After some discussion, he finds an outlet and plugs in his amp. The band members test their instruments and nod that they're ready to play. Dad takes a deep breath and announces, "Maria, I'm going to sing you 'Happy Birthday'!" I look at him. No comment.

Smiling at his fellow musicians that included the woman conga player, a rarity in 1973, my father taps the side of his timbales, yells, "*¡Uno, dos, tres, cuatro!*" and starts singing: "*¡Cumpleaños Feliz!*" tap, tap, tap, "*¡Cumpleaños Feliz!*" tap, tap, tap, tap, tap, "*¡Cumpleaños Maria!*"

Everyone is now on the dance floor, yelling, "*Vaya* Mambo! Just like the old times!" I continue to just stand in place and watch. Finally I go to Mami and ask why were they calling him Mambo.

"That was his stage name," she says.

Stage name? What else did I not know about him? About her?

A lot it would turn out. Tonight was just the beginning of things I didn't know or understand about my parents.

The song ends, and everyone is clapping and yelling that Mambo "still has it." He thanks them and asks for a cold beer, which is promptly fetched. Sweating and smelling of English Leather, he comes over to me and takes my hand.

"You know you look like her," he says, pointing with his nose at Mami.

"That's funny because she says I look like you," I reply.

He lets go of my hand and heads back to his band. Mami calls out to him and he comes over, bending down towards her face. She whispers something in his ear. He whispers something in return. Walking back to his trio he talks to them for a bit and they nod their heads in agreement.

Papi slowly puts down his drumsticks as the horn and conga player begin a song. Mami slowly rises from the wheel chair and takes the rubber hose of the oxygen tank out of her nose. She walks over to him, pain forgotten. Papi holds out his hand and my parents start to cha-cha. Someone yells out, "They're dancing. I haven't seen that in years!"

And it's happening at my Sweet Sixteen.

When the song finishes, my mother is having trouble breathing, but I could tell that she had enjoyed herself immensely. Soon after, she announces that she can't stay and needs to be taken back home. Several people volunteer to help her and within minutes she is gone. The party continues, but feels a little anti-climatic. More people start leaving as they wish me Happy Birthday again. I go searching for my father and find him sitting at the top of stairs looking downcast, beer bottle in hand. He is crying.

"I didn't know Rosie was sick. Why didn't anybody tell me?"

"She didn't want you to know."

He takes a swig of beer. I stare into nothing

"Your mother is the only woman I will ever love," he says.

Little did I know that tonight was the last time I would see my parents together. Or see them dance.

Part Two

The day I forgave my parents

Was the day I started to grow up

Three P.M.

You left on a hot humid New York City summer
day

After a long battle with an incurable disease

After you realized it was time to go.

At three p.m.

Your dancing days over.

Palladium, Hunts Point Palace, The Latin
Quarter.

How do I keep you alive?

You left on a hot humid New York City summer
day

Left me to go forward into the unknown.

Like Alice down the rabbit hole.

Landing in a world upside down.

At three p.m.

No Idea

After Mami's funeral, things got real. I didn't want to leave the only home I knew on 117th Street & Second Avenue. After all the years of taking care of Mami, everyone around me treated me like I knew what I was doing, like everything was back to normal. Rarely was I asked how I felt, if I was okay. Everyone had their own private revolution to deal with. Or whatever.

So at the age of sixteen, I had to learn how to take care of myself. But I had no idea what that meant. I was on my own. My father? Still missing in action.

It was the summer of '73 and I began hanging out with friends whose mothers made sure I had a hot plate of food, their *"Ay benditos"* handed out generously. Folks found it fascinating that I was an only child. I mean, how can I be a Puerto Rican girl and be an only child? That was, abnormal. "You sure you don't have a brother or sister around?" people would ask.

The thing about growing up without Mami is that I came to feel like an outsider. Every visit to my friends was met with that look: "She's the one that lost her mother," followed by a pregnant pause, the kind that in a play can throw off a whole scene. So without fully realizing what was happening, I stopped talking about my mother altogether. I became a loner, the outsider. I would go to my friend's home and watch them enjoy having their parents, feeling like the guest they knew deep down inside would leave soon.

I stopped crying, too, because after awhile people who hadn't shared my pain, hadn't experienced my loss, simply could not relate to me. My tears made them uncomfortable. They didn't know how to react, how to be.

The only time I could cry was listening to the song, "I'll Always Love My Mama" by The Intruders, which was a big hit that summer, playing on radio stations all over the FM dial, my favorite being WBLS. But in time, even that song became too much. Brought back the pain I was trying to forget. So I closed up my feelings. Shut them down as the best way to survive. Pretended I could handle it.

That strategy lasted me two years. Then came news of my father.

I'll try

The hospital wing where they put you looks like an old cave with faded chipped yellow walls.

As I walk in to see you again, your now feeble voice cries, *"Mi hija!"*

The tattoo on your left arm is visible. Yet somehow it seems faded too, even the part with my birth date. Like we're both disappearing.

I look at you with anger, that 18-year old anger of a teenager still mourning over her mother. You pat the bed and ask me to sit down, your liver two steps from getting ready to explode. The doctor had warned you had to stop drinking.

I look at your bloated stomach—the doctors call it "extended"—and you raise a shaky hand.

Shaky hands. I know them well by now, how they desperately grabbed a brown paper bag, you trying to be a gentleman by pouring the brown elixir in the cap of the pint, calling it a "shot," something to "calm my nerves."

Shaking hands. Looking like beaten highways—going nowhere—a sigh, a tear, a disappointment.

"Pour me some juice, *hija*," you ask.

I open the top, and the fumes of booze hit my nose.

I glare at you.

"I know I shouldn't. I'm in a hospital but..."

I refuse to serve you and call the nurse.

You get angry with me.

I get angry with you.

I get up to leave.

You yell out, "I'll try. I promise!"

As I wait for the elevator, I think about how much I wish I could believe you.

Night Fires

It was hot that night, the smell of fires strong despite the distance. We sat by the window, the one near the fire escape with a view of Bruckner Boulevard, watching the buildings burn like furnaces. It was the summer of 1977, July 13, and New York City was experiencing a citywide blackout.

I loved Abuela's face, perfectly round with small dimples, skin the color of dark toast, green eyes darting back and forth like a pendulum. I never liked looking at her directly. She made me feel naked, as if she could peer into my very soul. Still, I was her favorite, her first grandchild from her favorite son. Abuela lit another Virginia Slim cigarette and, in a measured voice, began talking to me about my life, my future, my journey.

My grandmother was a Curandera/Spiritualist/Santera all wrapped into one. In one moment she could look at you—or not look at you—as if you didn't exist, and in the next moment make you feel like the most important person in the world. She knew what I was thinking before I said it. She carried the family history in the center of her third eye. Although she smiled often, it invariably appeared with a slight shade of sorrow around her mouth. It must have been hard carrying the family spiritual burdens and not be able to tell everyone what their lives were going to be, or how it would turn out.

You see, Abuela's gifts, her sight was not wrapped up in how many beads she wore, or how many cigars she smoked, or how many fiestas for her Santos she had. Her gift was as simple as placing a glass of water on a table, and gazing at it to see the future. All the women on that side of the family were like that. But it came with a price. After all, truth, real truth can either set you free or make you plain crazy. With Abuela, time and experience taught her to just tell enough for the person to figure it out.

But on the evening of the New York blackout, July 13, her visions weren't about others. They were about me. As fires burned and the sound of shattered glass echoed in the streets of the Bronx, we could literally feel the community's anger: a hot soup of poverty, racism, and hunger boiling over. Nobody seemed interested in turning down the flame on the stove. And in that madness, my grandmother sat and slowly smoked her Virginia Slim, elegantly attached in her cigarette holder with a Japanese design, her pinky finger up in the air. Yes, she was that kind of lady, a snapshot from a 1940's film.

Abuela turned slightly and with her free hand gently pulled my face toward her.

"Mija, tengo mucho que decirte. Tu vida va a tener muchos caminos y ninguno va a ser seguro. Lo más difícil será cuando yo no esté aquí como hoy, pero yo voy a estar contigo siempre."

My heart began beating rapidly. I'd just turned twenty that year. It was the Disco Era, the age of Salsa and everything Fania. I had been living with my mother' sister in the Polo Grounds in Harlem after Mami passed away. It wasn't the best of circumstances and I knew I wouldn't stay there. I was a Voyager Daughter, the great wanderer never staying in one place too long, forever displaced, constantly reminded by my Aunt Ida that I was Rosie's-daughter-that-had-to-be-taken-in-after-my sister-died. Like a reason that always needed to be explained.

All this my Abuela knew as she inhaled her cigarette. I inhaled right along with her because by then I was smoking cigarettes too, Newports, and would have loved to bum a cigarette from her. But I didn't. I just sat and listened.

In a calm voice she explained how in Puerto Rico she was labeled "*una bruja*" because of her gift and how one time this woman accused her of stealing my grandfather from his wife. Abuela started laughing as if reliving the memory. As we watched the fires outside the window, she reminisced about how her house was set on fire in Puerto Rico and she had to make her way to New York. I did a double take. I just couldn't picture her doing that and told her so. She continued her story and said how funny it was that the women who would come to her on Saturdays for *consultas* would then go to Church on Sundays and pray. I didn't quite understand her point, but I remained quiet and listened. As the city was ablaze and rioting, Abuela seemed to be purging herself also. She finished her cigarette and returned her attention to me.

"Eres como tu papá y tu mamá. Cabeza dura. Pero también tienes un corazón de oro, y como tu Papá, vas a pasar mucho en la vida. No vas a tener paz hasta que llegues a mi edad."

As hard headed as my parents? Heading for a hard life and wouldn't find peace until I was almost her age? Not exactly what I wanted to hear at age twenty. Where was the nice story about how I would meet a nice husband? Fall in love, have kids and, well, like they say in the fairy tales and love songs, "Live happily ever after?"

I looked at her and asked, "Why?"

She put away her pack of cigarettes and told me that she knew that I smoked, but that she wasn't going to give me a cigarette anyway.

"Bad habit," she said.

Abuela walked over to the stove and asked if I wanted coffee, adding something about how her Santo wanted coffee at that moment. Whenever she talked like that I always looked around waiting to see if someone would magically appear out of thin air. Sipping Café Bustelo at the kitchen table, we sat in silence for a long time, waiting for the evening storm to pass.

The following morning, we could see plumes of smoke trailing up into the sky. But also with the dawn came a feeling I would remember for the rest of my life. Something had passed between Abuela and me, something meant only for us. As the city started its slow crawl back to normal, shop owners assessing the damages to their property, I got ready to head home. Power restored to the city, the elevated train rumbled along on Westchester Avenue.

When Abuela hugged me, I could see that her eyes were misty. She asked that I come by every Saturday, that it was important for us to keep talking. It would be years before I'd realize it, but those visits would become my first introduction to the family spiritual inheritance, a legacy that would be with me for the rest of my life.

Searching
(After Papi died)

The hole in my soul is
bottomless.

My younger life spent
constantly looking for
you

Around corners,
alleyways, crossroads,
railroads

Walking back to old
neighborhoods

Trying to retrace your
steps

Asking questions and
getting no answers

Listening to made-up
stories

Trying to glean some
sense of resemblance

An identity that
connected me to you

Daughter to father

Cobwebs of memory
blocked the sunlight

Until one day I grew so
tired that I realized

I would never find you
again

You have become a
phantom of my dreams

A dream walker in the
night

Part Three

There are too many people healing from old wounds

to inflict new ones.

Papi's Hands

Papi stories were for the telling over Christmas dinners. Laughter, inside jokes about how funny he was, proud of taking care of his sister's kids, all girls. Cousins sharing versions of Tío Victor playing horsey and carrying them on his back in the park; joking about his cravings for his sister's *sancocho,* that thick delicious homemade soup full of root vegetables, the special recipe passed down from mother to daughter all the way from Puerto Rico. The *sancocho* settled his stomach after a heavy night of drinking, and he'd always say how much he "really needed that," only to go out and do it all over again.

One evening, after several rounds of memories and laughter, my aunt looks at me and says: "You have your father's hands."

I look down at my hands, trying to picture his. A slight memory arrives of his long fingers grabbing and twirling drumsticks. My fingers are long. Are they the same as his?

"Your father always took care of his hands," she continues. Do I take care of mine? I wonder. Finger showing only knuckle? No hand cream?

I look at my aunt helplessly. No memory of Papi in that way.

"You have your father's hands," she repeats.

I look at mine. "I don't remember."

Flipping back her dark wavy hair she responds, "Well I do!"

"It must be nice to be his sister," I say.

She goes back to the kitchen table and the family remembrances start up again, laughing heads bobbing like a shared secret.

I look at my hands again, my strongest memory being one of a little girl not really interested in looking at her father's hand. She was just happy to be holding them.

Five Years

The self-imposed silence was mandatory to protect the fragile sprit that resided in my soul.

The battery of questions that came when I was asked about my parents:

"You mean you lost BOTH your parents?"

"Yes."

"Oh my God, that must be so hard on you! And you're an only child?"

"Yes."

"Are you sure you don't have any brothers or sisters?"

"Yes."

"Aren't you lonely? I mean you must be lonely?"

"I get by."

"Do you have other family?"

"Yes."

"Oh so it's okay then! I mean you have family!"

Internal Voice: *I just told you my parents are dead! And all you can say its' okay because I have family?*

The uncomfortable pause and then here it comes.

"I don't know what I would do if I was your age and lost my parents. *¡Dios Mio!* I would just die!"

Last conversation before I stopped talking about my parents. For five years.

First Month's Rent

It's a small studio in Elmhurst Queens, New York, but it's yours. Finally. Something in your own name.

You had promised to call your Abuela once you moved in, so you walk back to Roosevelt Avenue near the number 7 train and find a phone booth on the corner. Playing with the dime in your hand you insert the coin and dial.

"Hello? Mami?"

You'd taken to call your grandmother Mami. It felt right now.

"Bendición, mija," she says. *"¿Llegaste bien?"*

"Sí."

"Yo no sé por qué tenías que mudarte a Queens. ¡Es muy lejos!"

"Mami, era el único apartamento que estaba disponible.

"Okay. ¿Comiste?"

"No. Voy comprar algo ahora."

"Me llamas mañana ¿okay?

"Si, Mami. Bendición"

"Bendición, mija, y que Dios te acompañe."

Hanging up the phone, you stay in the booth as it hits home. You are on your own, all the way in Queens, a long way from the Bronx.

You cross the street and find a grocery store, where you buy a Swanson frozen chicken dinner. Coming out of the store, the roar of the 7 train rolls by and you realize this will be your new commute to work in Manhattan.

Opening the door to your new apartment, you are reminded that you have no furniture, including no bed to sleep in. The few boxes you packed are piled in the middle of the room. Luckily, Con Ed has turned the power on. Going through the boxes, you dig out the clock radio, the one purchased at Alexander's Department Store and plug it into the wall. Turning on the radio, the sounds are garbled with stations overlapping each other. Telling yourself to be patient, you find your favorite station, WBLS. McFadden and Whitehead are singing, "Ain't No Stopping Us Now."

Kicking a box out of the way, you start singing and dancing, the song's lyrics intended just for you. Amazing how it came on at this very moment. When the song is finished, you head to the kitchen and figure out how to turn on the oven. You heat your TV dinner and eat.

Sitting on the floor with no furniture and no bed, you look around and say aloud, "How am I going do this?" Indeed.

Getting up, you place the empty tinfoil tray that housed your chicken and mashed potatoes and green peas into the sink, to wash and use later. You comb the boxes, find your comforter and pillow, and make a make shift bed. It's time to settle in. To sleep on the floor of your first apartment.

Outside

Living on the abyss

Watching from the edge

Life goes by

Gingerly.

If you reach out you can touch the bubble

That was once your life.

The colorful chaos

The music loud

You're living on abyss

Watching from the edge

Trying to find a way back

Into the bubble

Real

The bottle rolls across the wooden floor sounding hollow, with an airy ringing sound enclosed. The aftertaste of rum is coated on your tongue and roof of your mouth. You watch the bottle continue its short ride as glass and floor meet. Again. They're not strangers.

It's become routine: bottle and you on floor, your face flat against the surface, enjoying the feel of cold on cheek, knowing that getting up was not going to be pleasant, not knowing how you got there. You gradually rise, startled to find you're still in your work clothes from the day before. It dawns on you that it's the middle of the week. You have to get to work.

What time was it? How did I get here? What the hell am I doing on the floor? The questions are familiar.

You attempt to sit up, the pounding in your head like an ambulance siren. Your body is filled with lead. You have to pee.

Slowly you gather your bearings and race to the bathroom, just in time to throw up your guts. Again. *God, I hate to vomit.* The emptiness in the pit of your stomach feels as if someone inserted a hot iron there. *I really have to get this checked. Must be getting an ulcer.*

Your mind wanders back to the bottle on the floor. *When did I buy that? And why did I get a fifth? I usually get a quart.* You vaguely recall getting off the train and stopping at a nearby liquor store. That's when you brought the fifth of rum, to go with the Chinese food you were buying. A lousy combination but who cares? Living alone allows for all sorts of strange habits.

Okay, time to stop the wandering mind and face reality, namely that I'm in no condition to go to work today. Coming out of the bathroom, you shuffle to the wall phone in the kitchen and call your supervisor. The conversation isn't pleasant. You've already missed work a few times this month. But your well-practiced nice voice sells her the bullshit that's you've come down with the flu, that "something was going around." What an actor you are!

Your boss instructs you to feel better and try and come in tomorrow. As always they were "short on staff." You thank her for understanding, hang up, and stare at the phone. *Lime green. Who the hell puts lime green phones in the kitchen?*

Taking a deep breath that doesn't smell so good when you exhale, you put a pot of coffee on the stove, and open the fridge. *Shit! Nothing to eat! Again. Wait a sec, there's some bread and margarine there. That'll have to do.*

As the coffee brews and the margarine softens, you return to the bathroom and take a hot shower, the water soothing your body's aches and pains. You notice a deep black and blue bruise on your left thigh. *Where did that come from?* This time, the memory bank comes up empty.

By the time the shower was over it didn't matter. All you want to do is to sit at your glass dining table, drink your cup of Café Bustelo, and eat your slice of Wonder Bread with melted Blue Bonnet Margarine. But the food doesn't relieve the bad headache that has refused to go away since you peeled yourself off the floor. Time for some aspirin to get through the day. You glance around the apartment and the questions return full force. *Why is the bottle of rum near the wall? Why is it empty? How did I get that nasty bruise? Was the Chinese food good?*

Enough, you tell yourself. The aspirins are calling and that's more important than worrying about an empty rum bottle on the floor. *Or is it?*

11/17

The meeting is on the Upper West Side of Manhattan. When you got up that morning the knots in your stomach were different. For ninety days there had been no more waking up on the floor; no more trying to patch together memories of the night before. Maybe that "One Day at a Time" mantra held some worth. You still felt like shit a few times, although the shakes had subsided considerably. Part of you still doubted whether you would ultimately succeed.

Walking into the meeting, you fight your usual urge to bolt out the door. After greeting the new friends you've made, you grab a cup of coffee and sit down. Most of the people in the room know how you feel. They've been there too.

But today you're especially nervous and scared because you're going to get your ninety-day coin. Who knew that all these years later you would be sitting a room with others like you?

The meeting nears the part celebrating your achievement. You're amazed that there are people in the hall celebrating *years* of being sober. And they're happy! You feel a momentary pang of jealousy, wondering how the hell they've done it. Then the mantra comes back in your head: "One Day at a Time." Yeah, that's how they did it. And that's how you'll do it.

Finally your name is called. You walk to the front of the room, state your name, and are handed the coin. Clutching it like a lifesaver, you see that it reads: "To Thine Own Self Be True."

You squeeze the coin in your hand so hard that you wonder if it'll leave a permanent imprint.

The meeting ends. The dozen or so people gathered there congratulate you again. After the last cup of coffee is poured, everyone is ready to go home. You get that familiar pain in the pit of your stomach again, the one that tells you it's time to go home too. Alone. You thank everyone and leave.

On the train ride back home, holding on to the coin for dear life, you start another internal conversation with God, this time asking if this is right and should you continue? That maybe it's okay to a drink once in a while and, hey, can you really be expected never to drink the traditional Puerto Rican alcohol-based eggnog called *cocoquito* on Christmas day? Ever?

At home, the fridge is stocked with healthy food. As you're figure out what to prepare, you check out the calendar on the kitchen wall to note the date of your ninety-day milestone. You gasp as the tears well up. It is November 17, the day your father died in 1979. The day you became like an orphan.

The memories of the day sweep you in a tidal wave of emotions. You hear clearly his voice calling you, *"¡Mi hija!"* You hear clearly the promises to stop drinking. And then you think of your own promises, the ones to yourself.

You crumple to the floor and for the first time, you cry for your Father.

Part Four

My Nuyorican Puerta

&

Open Mics

First time at Nuyorican Poets Café

Storefront with beat- up bar

I enter midday/midweek

tattered paper

words written unevenly

fragmented, misspelled

a carved moment of someone else's life.

Or maybe mine on a train from the Bronx.

I had heard

there was a place where Puerto Ricans gathered

to read poetry.

The Nuyorican *puerta* opened.

Elegua tells me, "Walk through."

And I did.

Finding a smoked-filled room

poetic voices gathering

a communal tribe

where I could speak my truth, my Spanglish.

Where fingers snapped "*¡Vaya!*" and "*¡Así es!*"

Instead of: "Shut up!" Or "Girls don't talk like that!"

Where there was pride in our history. My history.

A Puerto Rican woman ready to do battle.

The Nuyorican *puerta* opened on a Friday night.

Elegua told me, "Walk through."

And I did.

TIRED

I am tired of explaining myself

Who I am

Where I'm from

Who are/were my parents

Explaining

My culture

My language

Spanish

Spanglish

English

Any "ish" way of talking.

Tired of hearing the same old questions that

 Justify

Criticize

Verify

Rectify

Clarify

Marginalize

So I can

Fit

Fit

Into some form of acceptance

Tired of not being the "perfect Latina" you see

On film, telenovelas

And God forbid that a brown/black

No- hair woman should be a Latina

Of your persuasion

Because although you won't admit it out loud

It's not permissible.

Tired of being

Intellectualized

Written with such academic clarity

That the essence of my soul/ being

Is reduced to an academic footnote

Tired of being told to branch out

Change my language for others

When so few of us

Have a unique voice

That carries over the centuries of

Subjugation

Segregation

Separation

I am tired

So therefore

For every question I am asked

I will look you in the eye

Speak my truth

Listen to my soul because

I had to learn to be my own

Teacher

Mother

Father

Sister

Brother

Elder

Grounded

Rooted to earth

Water

Light

Because that's the way

I discovered

Who I am

How I am.

South Bronx in Black & White

*Inspired by "Seis de Sur" Photography Exhibit Bronx
Documentary Center, 2013.
Dedicated to: Francisco Molina Reyes II, Angel
Franco, Joe Conzo Jr.,
David Gonzalez, Edwin Pagan, & Ricky Flores.*

Time and place in gritty black & white

photographs

a South Bronx that is no longer present.

Rubble, burning buildings

broken hydrants

water spilling into hot tar

blood running into baked streets.

Abuelas blessing *tecatos*

hookers turning tricks to live/survive

children being children

running around with plastic water guns

good cop/bad cop.

Generational dancing still grinding, sashaying

hips to the hot beat step of clave.

salsa in the middle of the streets

as long as the speakers worked

and records didn't get stuck.

Teenagers claiming their uniqueness

on beat up cardboard boxes

that would bloom like a flower

As break dancing was born and disco sounds

became abbreviated scratches on records

That back in the day were the hits of tech music

in clubs like the Garage, Loft and Tunnel

A beat and rhythm

Hip Hop.

Windows covered with graffiti

on trains "into the city"

where calling out the stations

became the duty of the passenger near the door.

Life went on.

Families were raised.

Children went to school.

Everyone not knowing that one day

they would become part of history.

That folks who weren't there

would look back with nostalgia

asking those that were there:

"What was it like?"

Part Five

In the end no matter what,

you have to learn to live with yourself.

Fifth Decade #1

Bunions

Sagging breasts the shape of upside down pears

Waistline gently shaped like a barrel

Eyes wrinkling

Lines deepening

Some days everything is a bother

The sight

The smell

The noise

The annoying people, young and old

The moving from one decade to another.

Yet, there is still dignity and grace

Pear shaped breast?

Change the bra

Bunion feet?

Buy the right shoes

Barreled shaped waistline?

Hey, that comes with time

Remember when it was 24 inches!

Lines on face?

Okay, it's still a good face

Wrinkled eyes?

A sign of wisdom and experience

This is a new decade

Where each step is a journey

Each door a choice

Each path a decision

Arriving at a destination and understanding

That everything in the Universe

Has its place.

Fifth Decade (addendum)

But when you get there

Walk the path slowly

Never compare it to others

Embrace what is around you

Get rid of what doesn't work

Accept change even when it is hard

Don't ignore yourself for others because

Then you are no good to others

Surround yourself with all things positive

You are going to need them.

Daughter to Mother

Loving laced words were not your strengths.

Gentleness in your voice seldom heard.

Giving orders was like giving directions for life.

You took away the innocence of childhood

And never realized it.

Treating life like a burden

Always angry at the hand dealt.

Regretting that you could not live the life you

wanted.

Your mantra: "You were born with three strikes

against you. You're Black, poor and uneducated.

You can take care of the last two but you will

always be Black."

Finally, in the end you could only say that I was a good Daughter.

Perhaps that was as close as to saying, "I love you."

But you see, l loved you too

Even though you were not an easy woman to love.

You were and still are my Mother.

Father to Daughter

You would always show up at the last minute.

Breaking promises.

I grew up hating that word.

You could never really look me in the eye

But your pride of having a daughter must have

given you peace of mind.

At least I like to think so.

I wasn't allowed to love you.

I was taught that you were the bad part of me.

I was taught not to be like you.

But I am you.

My heart beats with your clave

With bloodlines that flow from father to

daughter

With a clave beat that eventually would become

my own.

You never denied me. Some folks can't say that.

So, no you didn't give me the care and nurturing

that all daughters want from their fathers

But you gave me what you could.

You gave me life.

What more can I ask for?

I was and still am your daughter.

Con El Permiso

Taking out the old leather pouch lined with creases from the folds of life, you remove some tobacco and rub a pinch between your fingers. Opening your hand, the tobacco blows into the wind, a part of your ritual before chanting and asking the Caregivers of the Universe for permission to do healing work. At times, the ritual involves fire. Sometimes it's as simple as offering black dirt from the earth to the high winds of sky.

It is early evening in Coney Island, your childhood magical place transformed into a place of spirit. You sit on the sand and wait for your Ancestors to speak in forgotten languages that only bloodlines understand. And they do speak.

Just like your Abuela spoke to you all those years ago on Saturday afternoons, with cigar smoke circling her head and heart, and yours too eventually. Abuela would leave you one day, but not before gifting you with spirit, light, and hope.

You inhale deeply as the breath of life flows through your chest like an extra lung, the forces of nature pulling you back and forth as the Ancestors circle you. You have learned how to listen, how to see. It is a glorious feeling and your Ancestors dance in celebration that someone is still left in the present time to continue their work. At first they talk amongst themselves. Is she ready to know our secrets? Would she understand? Follow through with her journey? You listen to what was being said and not being said. After much discussion and dance, the Ancestors decide you are ready for change, to become a new person, unafraid of life and the challenges that await you.

The winds die down and the sun sets. You slowly get up and fold the leather pouch given to you by Abuela, a talisman to your past. Smiling you ignore the aches of joint and muscle. Smiling you remember all those years ago when Abuela told you that one day you would be happy when you reached her age and after 50 plus years, you are now at peace.

Thank You

I want to thank the wonderful editorial team of David Perez and Veronica Golos for again collaborating with me on my second book. I thank you for your dedication and clarity of vision. Your work as writers, artists, and the professionalism that you bring to my work will always be honored, respected and admired.

A deep appreciation goes to my dear Hermana Mia Roman Hernandez who again came on board with my second book and with loving care saw my vision, concept and created a loving cover honoring my parents. Mia's artwork continues to be exhibited around the country and her work as a Healing Artists continues to grow. I am grateful to have worked with this wonderful team of creative souls who always bring their light and good spirits to the work.

And finally to my husband Bobby Gonzalez, multicultural motivational speaker and national storyteller. You are always there for me. You are my heart.

About the Artist

Mia Roman Hernandez is an internationally known, award-winning Nuyuorican self taught artist, educator, illustrator and workshop facilitator. Born and raised in New York City, her artwork has been showcased in national and international exhibitions, art galleries, local community institutions and private collections. Mia's creative language of color, her medium for storytelling, if you would like more information about her work please visit her website at: www.artsbymia.com

About the Author

Maria Aponte is a Poet/Performance Artist/ Community Arts Activist/Educator. Maria works in Latino Theatre against racial discrimination and women's rights. She has written and performs her two one woman shows, *Lagrimas de mis Madres* an autobiographical play based on the women in her family, and *I Will Not be Silenced* based on the life of Sor Juana Ines de la Cruz. Maria performs her work at colleges/universities/ conferences locally and nationally. She has been featured on Bronx Net, News 12, NBC Latino and WABC-TV. Maria has been published in *The Marymount Review*, the literary magazine of Marymount Manhattan College.

She studied at the Iowa University Summer Writer's Workshop. Her one woman show, *Lagrimas de Mis Madres* was published by Marquette University and Western Michigan University in *Caribe Revista de Cultura y*

Literatura. She has been published in Phati'tude Literary Magazine's issue; ¿What's in a Nombre? Writing Latin@ Identity in America, The Nuyorican Women Writers Anthology published in Voices e/Magazine, the Center for Puerto Rican Studies, Hunter College- CUNY; an online literary journal, editor Dr. Nancy Mercado. In May 2013 Maria's first book, *Transitions of a Nuyorican Cinderella* won 2nd Place for Best Poetry in English at the International Latino Book Awards. *Transitions of a Nuyorican Cinderella* is listed on **RockThoseReads** selected books about Harlem by Total Equity Now. Maria has her Masters in Latin American/Latino Studies from Fordham University. She is a member of the PEN American Center. Maria is also the founder of Latina 50 Plus™ a program honoring Latina Pioneers. For information please visit Maria's websites at www.mariaaponte.com and www.latina50plus.com Twitter mamaponte@73

Authors Note

The illness that my mother Rosa Maria, passed away from is called Scleroderma, or systemic sclerosis, a chronic connective tissue disease generally classified as one of the autoimmune rheumatic diseases. At the time of her death in 1973, very little was known about the disease and was in the early stages of research. Today there is the Scleroderma Foundation if you would like more information please visit their website at www.scleroderma.org

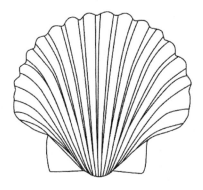

Made in the USA
Columbia, SC
14 May 2018